MW01292932

HAPPY AGAIN

Easy steps to fixing your relationship now

Susan Howard

Copyright @2018

All rights reserved. No part of this book may be reproduced in any form without writing permission in writing from the author. Reviewers may quote brief passages in reviews.

No part of this publication may be reproduced or transmitted in any form or by any means, mechanical or electronic, including photocopying or recording, or by any information storage and retrieval system, or transmitted by email without permission in writing from the publisher.

While all attempts have been made to verify the information provided in this publication, neither the author nor the publisher assumes any responsibility for errors, omissions or contrary interpretations of the subject matter herein.

This book is for entertainment purposes only. The views expressed are those of the author alone and should not be taken as an expert instruction or command. The reader is responsible for his or her actions.

Adherence to all applicable laws and regulations, including international, federal, state and local governing professional licensing, business practices, advertising, and all other aspects of doing business in US, Canada or any other jurisdiction is the sole responsibility of the purchaser or reader.

Neither the author nor the publisher assumes any responsibility or liability whatsoever on the behalf of the purchaser or reader of these materials. Any perceived slight of any individual or organisation is purely unintentional.

Please sign up for more free info at http://www.urbanlife.tips/

Table of contents

Why I Wrote This Book?

Relationships between us as couples are in trouble.

Are we actors who forgot the most important part we came out to play?

We have forgotten what it took us to find that special person and now it's all caught up in "if" and "don'ts." We have left our audience completely confused, and we still do not know how we got to this phase.

What started out as a desire to be cherished together have all become something we cannot fathom? The Society we live in today does not make it any less good with so much at stake, women feeling cheated, men feeling emasculated and no end in sight to all these tales of woes. Separation and Divorce is now a part of the contract signed before marriage and we all begin to wonder, are we better off alone?

How do you reconcile the happy faces at the Wedding ceremony with the embittered men and women we see in later years? How do we renew that enthusiasm in our relationships, so we do not end up that way? My only wish for you is to have the best relationship and enjoy great peace of mind and therefore if you have issues with your relationship, big or small, I will teach you how to solve it all.

I am not going to give you pretty words or judge you or make you feel bad. I will provide you with straightforward answers to problems you face every day, big or small.

Why Should You Read This Book?

The focus of this book will be on everything you need to reconnect with your partner.

I promise that you can change your relationship for the better, but all I need from you while reading this book is an open mind because every little thing that needs fixing in your relationship will be done through you and you alone.

You should read this book because it is the result of researches among couples and it summarizes everything that science knows about problems in relationships. Without too many details, I will identify and describe problems and offer solutions that work in a majority of cases.

As you go through this book, you must contemplate every page with concentration, you are not allowed to skim or scan, you are only allowed to read through this book with great determination and hope that the greatest gift of your friendship started this way.

Chapter One

Problems After Perfect Six Months

Relationships are perhaps the most controversial of issues; it is a single word loaded with so much. It is filled with implications, fears, uncertainties, joys, heartbreak, emotions and so much more.

We begin our relationships with dreams and aspirations, so many illusions, but soon it becomes much more than that that we can build stronger bonds or get broken. It is a double-edged sword, so complex and complicated. We can have financial abundance, strength in union, great kids or we can end up embittered and desolate. Whatever our relationship becomes is a matter of choice, but usually, this choice is an unconscious one.

Because Relationships are quite complex, some people prefer to skip the roller coaster and has placed having relationships at the bottom of their priorities. This is a misconception because the truth about this is that relationships are the center of our whole existence; it is your lifeline to health and happiness, a path to a higher purpose, a passport to greater peace and an outlet to success. There is no such thing as life without relationships and vice versa. Marital relationships are a great plus to our lives and only with an excellent understanding of its concept will you achieve an extraordinary relationship. It is important to note that extraordinary relationships are not borne out of luck, chemistry or convenience as is commonly believed, but is built accepting the laws and skills of love, practice and practicing until death.

These laws depend significantly on understanding on all three levels if we must achieve the best relationships, not just with our spouse, but with our kids, family, extended family, friends, and well-wishers. These three levels of understanding include:

- Cognitive understanding (knowledge at an intellectual level)
- Emotional understanding
- Understanding of physical nature of love

It is only until you have a complete understanding of all three levels that you can have that extraordinary relationship. But these understandings are not broken into these levels, No, they are found in the little things we do to make things right between each one of us.

Falling in Love

Falling in love is such a beautiful experience; it symbolizes the notion of moving from the stage of having only neutral feelings with the person of interest to feelings of love. We can fall in love over a long time or get strongly attracted at an instant. Falling in love, then can be described as being beautiful, terrifying, nauseating and often a roller coaster of emotions. When in love, we begin to see our partner as a unique individual, a soul mate; we focus wholly and unconsciously on our Partner's positive assets while understudying their flaws. We thrive and focus on all events and memories that remind us of our beloved. We daydream about few shared moments, and things we wish could happen in the future. This is why it is a roller coaster of emotions as it makes us dwell on euphoria, enhanced emotions. We lose appetite and the border between feelings of panic, anxiety, and despair when faced with an unpleasant moment with our partners. We are caught between feelings of vulnerability and strength.

Scientists have related the concept of falling in love with the secretion of certain chemicals in the brain and around the body, but nothing really explains that wholesome feeling. Love has reduced even the greatest of men to puppies and has made others much stronger. Yet, despite the fact that a lot of us have experienced this at one point, no one can fully state what happened that got us to the stage of problems or why we even fall out of love.

Why problems start

If love is such a beautiful thing, then why do we fall out of love?

Why do issues begin that creates these gaps?

A good understanding of why problems arise will help you rebuild your relationship.

It is crucial we start by saying that we are infinitely different, no two humans are similar, even Twins; the idea of having a roommate for life should be first addressed from this perspective. You cannot expect your partner to think like you, feel like you and discuss things the same way. Troubles usually arise when we make the mistakes of trying to turn our Partners into idealized versions. Yes, we probably began our relationships, focusing on the Positive traits, but now it's time to face the music and indeed accept your significant other; you are required not to try to change your partner but, to improve yourself.

Problems in relationships may arise from many different things, but the first step comes from you and requires identifying the source of all this ups and downs.

Past Experiences

Some of us have been through a whole lot in our lives. Baggage from past relationships, traumatic events as well as our previous environment may affect our relationship. Your parents may have been divorced, or you were subject to an abusive home. Such things may hinder you from really enjoying your relationship. As we go on, we will understand more and more about the root of all these problems.

Life transitions and stress

Sometimes passing through the phases may cause undue burden to our relationships. It could be as simple as adjusting to sharing space with each other, or as complex as having a baby. Long-term relationships could also pass through stress when children leave home, or retirement or the loss of a loved one. Financial issues may also affect our relationships.

Embracing Myths

The idea of loving a person for the fact that they "complete you" is foolhardy. Your partner only completes you when you truly understand each other and bearing in mind that as humans we undergo change every day and this will let you know that such a day will never come. There's no perfect woman or man, there's only flawed perfection. An ideal man or woman is either a Psychopath or a Martyr. We only achieve perfection when we truly understand how to adjust and accept our Partner for their flaws as well as their positive traits.

Behavioral factors

Our thought patterns are entirely different, and so is our reaction to heartbreaking scenarios. You may weep at an incredible sight, but your partner may not do the same.

You may be receptive to criticism, but your partner may grow defensive to them. Understanding each other's reactions may help bring you closer to each other.

How do I know I have a problem?

Every relationship has its ups and downs at some point, but how do you know when it is not working out? Sometimes, pronounced issues may arise which may enlighten you on the fact that your relationship is no longer working, but more often there are no such telltale signs. Other specific problems may seem minimal, but if not corrected may lead to more significant issues.

There is no significant list of ways to know if your relationship is going through a phase or on the verge of breaking up. Some publications we see today tell us that if your conflicts are so much more, then you too have some issues to settle. Sometimes you may not have any disputes, but may break up in the future and at other times you may have conflicts and still adore each other. The best approach to defining the level of peace in your relationship only starts by analyzing yourself and this will be discussed subsequently.

Chapter Two

Identifying Your Problems

Reconnection is no small feat and requires a lot of open wounds for both you and your partner. Each time I encounter people who say their relationship is leading nowhere; I get them quiet by a simple question "define the problem in a single word." Each time, there is a pause which is then followed by ranting and ravings about how their partner has committed this or that. Often enough, it's very accurate, but more times, it's also a problem instigated by them both. There's no such thing as a one-sided relationship, there's only a two-fold interaction. Usually, defining the problem is a bit difficult as we often let pride and ego get in the way of looking inwards.

Sorry, it can't work that way! You need to let go of all that emotions and take a clear and objective view of all the assets and liabilities that led to the stage you both are in. More than half your problem will be solved by defining the problems.

Defining the problem is step one to the solution; you should sort out the root of it all.

- Is it what you did personally that brought about positive or negative attributes, have you helped it grow?
- Have you contributed to it?
- When you feel something is wrong with your relationship, can you pinpoint the exact problem or are you guessing based on instant emotional reactions to every perceived danger?
- Is it specifically a problem in your head or one you can objectively find?
- Is it your lack of expression, instant tendency to fight or your fear of closeness? Are you entirely sure you are not reacting solely to anxiety and fear or something you both should work on?
- Are these problems you both instigated together?

You should understand that treating your relationship is just like managing any other sickness; it requires a diagnosis, which can only explain the right method or pathway to the solution. If you arrive at the wrong diagnosis, then you know what that means, you won't find the correct answer.

The worst case scenario is when you use defective conclusions to sort problems in your relationship. To be able to perfect or improve your relationship, you are required to thoroughly and accurately analyze all little aspects of your relationship. You must dot all "I's" and cross all "t's" to completely rescue your relationship.

Let's talk about you

Your relationship begins with you; you are both your friend as well as your enemy. A good number of us pass through life without evaluating our true potentials, flaws and everything else that is part of our personality. As humans, you must understand that there is no mirror image of you out there, you remain infinitely you.

Your thought patterns, your reactions and most importantly, your perceptions make you what you are, and this influences your relationship. A good understanding of your flaws, likes, dislikes, and anything about you will prepare you for anything you will face in future. Let's take a good look at your innermost being to help us establish the bottom line.

You will need a pen and maybe a journal to carry out this analysis; I prefer this method as what is written on paper can be glaringly seen as what it really is.

Note: *Before you begin jotting down into that paper, you have to promise yourself that you tell the truth; this is not about retaining your relationship but becoming a better you. You must search deep down and fill only accurate information.*

Let's get started and use the method developed by Phillip McGraw in his Relationship Rescue (2000). This is a key part of SWOT method, but adjusted to personal use. The first step is to finish sentences below:

- If criticized I tend to...............
- I am happiest when I...........
- When I am angry I........
- I would be so happy if my partner will.........
- Sometimes I feel...........
- I would give more acceptances, if..........
- My father was...........
- My mother.........
- I only wish I had.....
- Growing up I was.....
- My best quality......
- Sometimes at night.....
- My worst flaw........
- I regret .... Part of my life
- When I do .... I feel I am fake
- My life took these turn when.........'
- I hate it when I...........................

- We laughed a lot each time I.......................
- It helps when we..........
- My partner fears the most when I..........
- My partner gets angry when.......
- I hate it when my partner does.........

Halfway through:

Now turn over the sheet and take a look at your answers, what do you find?

Who do you think you are? Honesty is exceedingly essential if you are to find the right answers.

To answer the next questions, place a true or false at the front of each item:

- I am satisfied with my sex life
- I never get attention from my partner
- I trust my partner
- I feel like a kid around my partner
- I do not have any plans towards the future for us
- "I Love you" only comes from my partner
- I see us separated
- We still have fun nights
- All I want to do at times is hurt my partner

- I am ashamed of my partner
- My partner is ashamed of me
- It's so boring these days being around my partner
- My partner treats me with respect
- My partner understands me
- I feel trapped
- I enjoy having the house to myself
- I find it hard talking about my feelings
- I demand appreciation
- I love being in control
- My partner is a taker
- My partner is jealous of me
- I feel needed by my partner
- I am not satisfied with my partner
- My partner should feel lucky to have me
- I feel always judged and rejected by my partner
- I feel like I am always compared to others
- I will never satisfy a partner
- My partner feels I am boring in bed

Listing it all

Now I want you to do real SWOT analysis of a nice abundant list of who you are, please note that you must have at least ten of each:

Flaws	Values
....	....
....	....
....	....
....	....

Dislikes	Likes
....	....
....	....
....	....
....	....

We will get back to you soon; I do hope you are not feeling too bad yet. Let's explore other factors. Remember, you are talented and valued, but with passing years, you have forgotten how much it feels to be happy. You deserve happiness, but I believe you can have that with your partner.

Communication

Communication has a lot of meanings to different aspects of life, but in all still talking about the same thing. Communication indicates having a mutual sharing with your partner. In more descriptive terms, marital communication is a constant exchange of accurate information in the form of messages involving speech patterns through mediums such as letter writing, phone, facial expression, body contacts and so on.

To add more quality to our definition; Communication involves the capacity to adequately express one's feelings, desires and beliefs to another in a way that it is understood, acknowledged and responded by the receiver.

When we are united and decide to be in a relationship or marriage, we enter into a position that is burdened with dangerous spots.

According to Victor Salz, "marriage is a time of great fighting in which there is less involved with the world and more with each other. This author is underlining that marriage was characterized by the struggle and the importance of learning how to fight fairly.

We have to learn to make out imaginary rules if we are determined to get along properly. Without these set of rules, a lot of things may go wrong. I do not mean setting ridiculous standards such as you should do this or that, but regulations that embody love as the solution to every problem or obstacle faced in your relationship. But to set these rules, what is the level of communication in your relationship?

Why then do you feel the need to curb your sexual activity with your partner? A lot of us carry the excuse of being too tired to initiate such contact because we had a hectic day.

I do have a busy day too, but I developed this mindset. " I do love a good night sleep and sleeping off after much stress in the day doesn't actually relax me, so Sex ends my day, no matter the hour." Since Sex will give you better sleep patterns and increase intimacy, why do you do away with it?

To make matters much worse, some of us reading this book at this time will have more excuses to give about the importance of sex to the relationship.

However, a lot of us do have a lot of sex with our spouse, but there are no emotions attached, it's all a matter of business or procreating. To understand the chemistry between you and your spouse, let's take a good look at it via this way:
- I am still physically attracted to my spouse
- My partner makes me feel sexy at all times
- Sex with my partner is enthusiastic and sufficient
- My partner always flirts with each other
- My partner and I love being alone with each other rapped under the sheets

- My partner and I still look each other in the eye when talking or alone
- If my partner and I do not have sex every few days, I miss it so much
- I enjoy looking at my partner's body
- I am most pleased when I give my partner physical pleasure

If you have much more favorable answers, then "cynically" you are in the clear. But if you do have a lot more negative responses, then we have to work it out later in this guide.

Money

Money is a significant problem in lot of our relationships. Most often we feel our partners are spending a lot more than us in some way. This is an excellent avenue for arguments. But how do you curb these issues? A good number of homes are laden with this issue. For men, it's worrying that their wives spend so much on facials, beauty, and fashion, and for women, it is a whole different scenario. It's even much worse if the woman, in this case, is a stay-at-home mom. It is good you understand that money can make or your mar your relationship.

Some of us believe that since money can ruin our relationship, then it's better to keep separate bank accounts. Well, this is so wrong; you can keep different bank accounts and still pick fights.

Picture this:
You had a great day at the selling of a house in the neighborhood and received a nice bonus; you decided to take yourself shopping and got a really expensive outfit only because you could afford it. What do you think your spouse will say about it when you got back?

There are probably many different answers and reactions that should be expected, and most of them actually will be a surprise, jealousy and most importantly, anger, therefore, do you still think a separate bank account is a solution?

Picture again a different scenario:
"It's your partner's birthday, and you can't seem to know what to get him/her. Since you both share a joint account, it's not quite as easy. Let's say you settle for that nice over the top gift, why can't you, since you bring in much more. What will your partner say once he/she sees "feeding money" wrapped up in a different package?"

Both scenarios are seen every day and have led to a lot of breakups; The truth is there is no right method of keeping your money, there exists only understanding.

Dividing labor at home

In the US, according to a Poll in 2007(3), it was discovered that the division of labor ranked third after sex and faithfulness in the list of things that led to breaking up among couples. A lot more of us are working this day and its good you understand what I mean by working, we all are, whether you are a stay at home mom or you have a business to run, you are working. The only difference between both scenarios is that one of them is bringing in some of the money. Some of us do get a helper, someone to help out with the household chores. This is an excellent solution if only it were that simple. Soon, problems will likely arise since you are doing all the work.

Take a step back from your emotions and check yourself out. What is the reason you spend more time embittered and angry? Are you sure it's not because you are the only one in charge of taking care of the house? You do have to sort it out if this is the issue. Take out the journal once again and try as much as possible to list out those areas of your marital journey that is handled just by you. It's going to hurt a bit, but we have to get it all out on paper if this book works for you.

For a woman starting out your home, please never make the mistake of taking it all on your shoulders only because it's just the two of you, once you start a family, it can be a bit harder to change routine already set in stone.

Every marital conflict including infidelity arises from every bit of the problems listed here. You now have a journal filled with issues you have to tackle. Since we have been able to find the root of our problems, the solution is now in sight. All it takes is a bit of dedication and patience, and soon you will be able to inspire a whole lot of positive things into your relationship.

But while using this book, never you think you can control your partner, except it's an integrated approach, you can only work on yourself.

The reality is that working on yourself can improve your relationship and as much improve your partner's approach towards you. And never should you feel you need your partner to enhance your life. Remember, you are responsible for your actions!

Chapter Three

Mapping Out The Solution To Your Problems

After going through each of the problems outlined in the previous chapter, I know you must feel really desolate and more like a terrible person. Some of you may even feel wholly righteous right now. If you do feel that way, please go back and start this book again because I think you scanned through it and obviously did not get the message.

For those of you who feel really bad right now, do understand that your relationship is just the same as every other relationship out there. The only difference is your lack of management.

Successful couples have problems, this is because we are human beings and come with different needs and desires. The only difference between you and those successful couples is that they make do with every flaw and every vice and try as much as possible to make their relationship work well.

There is no such thing as relationship cure or fix, there is only relationship management.

- How do you manage each obstacle that comes between the both of you?
- How do you manage your finance, death of a loved one, the birth of a new child, parents' issues, and school issues? There are a whole lot of them that will come at every day you two wake up next to each other.
- How do you manage your relocation, the loss of your job or contract?
- How do you relate to your partner at the down times and uptimes?

All these and more have influences in your relationship. Work on all aspects, and whenever problems arise, you will be in a capable position to take control of it all.

Personalizing the solution

It's time we dealt with issues personally; we cannot afford to contaminate our relationship any longer. We have to start contributing to its growth. It's time you took the initiative and developed you into a great personality. It's time to activate the positive traits and limit the negative. It's time to get rid of all wrong emotions and embrace a better lifestyle. You have to reach inwards and extract your unique and beautiful self. To do this, we will incorporate 10 steps to personal upliftment. These steps will give you a better approach towards everything you are to contribute to your relationship. It's time to take a bold step towards living with more integrity, dignity, honesty, compassion, and enthusiasm. When you do change your outlook towards your relationship, you will be able to achieve that balance in your life.

Step 1: Own Your Relationship

Every little thing in your relationship, both the ups and downs had your hands tied in it. So it's time you told yourself the truth, you own your relationship, and so you are responsible for every baggage that comes with it. Owning up to this fact means you accept responsibility for all altitudes and reactions. You have to understand that all that nagging, whining and anger has influenced your relationship. Yes, it can be justified, but you have to accept there may have been better approaches. Accept that you contributed to the troubles you see today and after that, you will be prepared to take the next step in the direction of better days.

Step 2: Vulnerability is part of it all: Accept it

The risk is obvious, being in love means taking the risk of having your heart dashed to pieces. You can't say you love someone and then you tell tales of leaving some of it for yourself. Well, it will not work that way. When you like someone, you bare your heart to them. I know each time you are faced with any problems in your relationship that you do react with two basic emotions; Fear and anxiety.

It is a natural situation, but what should make it different is the way you choose to control your feelings. Do you let feelings of betrayal and fear become the driving factors towards your outward reactions or do you take a pause and try some other method? Take a different method instead of reacting like a time bomb. Tell yourself this- "if my partner does something negative that hurts me when I open up and care about him again, I will survive, I will sit back and keep trying until I get it right."

Step 3: Accept your partner

A lot of us enter into relationships with a mythical mindset. We have idealized versions of our partners taking no records of their flaws. This is particularly natural since at the onset, love sort of keeps your eyes from all those flaws. But now, you know your partner, it's time to accept them for who they are. Acceptance is essential for a relationship to go on. The spirit of acceptance is vital for reconnection. Back off on all that criticism, mockery and undue judgment. Yes, they may be sloppy, unattractive or not as ambitious as you are. You should remember one thing; you are together because you are different. Some of us profess to love someone and then add it up with "if only he/she were like this, l would love more." It is so easy to see relationships out there where there's so much energy spent on "what ifs" instead of focusing on the virtues of one another. No one is perfect, and you can only strive to attain perfection, but there's no such thing as an ideal man or woman.

Get off trying to change your partner and build a character of acceptance. You will be amazed at the reactions you will witness then.

Step 4: Focus on friendship

Friendship is foundational to every relationship and most likely started out as such. But due to the strain and stress caused by letting your emotions run haywire, you have forgotten how to be friends. Well, it's time to rekindle that friendship. Remember all that things you used to admire when you started out and work towards having them again. It will not be easy, but it is essential. Recapture that energy you spent in making your relationship the first time, do this without looking at the problems or trying to compare both scenarios. All you have to do is work towards it. Remember something made you decide to make a go of this relationship, build it up again. Was it the movies that you shared reviews about, or was it lunch? Whatever you did back then, bring it all back. Go out and have fun as friends would and not as lovers with a lot of baggage. Do note that when you started out, you were probably polite to each other as is often seen in friendships. Work on this and watch how things begin to take a newer better form.

Step 5: Promote your partner's self-esteem

Okay, I know this looks a bit dubious. Apparently, you feel this plan is ridiculous. I have asked you to take a risk, accept and then be a friend, now I am saying you should praise your partner.

Yes, you must appreciate being appreciated. Pick up the journal again, and list out all those beautiful things about your partner. Now even when you do not feel like it, you will have to appreciate it, and you have to do this verbally. Also, when you feel they have offended you, instead of trying out a formula that will make them feel deflated, why not restructure the statement to look like this " I cannot tolerate this behavior of yours because I believe you are a much better person." Most often, you may be right about something, but your words may hurt so bad that your partner will take the defensive. So no matter how much you wish to criticize, always bear this in mind: your partner's self-esteem takes the first position before that criticism.

Step 6: Direct your frustrations properly

Sometimes, we get so frustrated with circumstances that we do not care who gets a bit of the cake. Never transfer one matter to another. You have problems just like everyone else including your partner, but they may handle this differently. Do not vent it out on them merely because they are so close by. Take a step back from your issue and objectively deal with them. Sometimes, you may be entirely clueless about how much your frustrations are unjust, especially when you feel your partner contributes to it. One thing you should learn to do is to be emotionally honest with yourself at all times. Find the problem or the root of your problem from an objective view and then find the solution. Do not fight your partner as if he/she were the enemy. You only deny yourself a chance at happiness by such actions.

Step 7: Be straightforward

Actively communicating your problems with your partner is an excellent way to begin healing. Whenever you feel hurt by your partner, do not take the high road by incorporating malice or storing up emotions. Try to have a productive session with your partner and sort out things together. Everyone has a whole different set of feelings, and you should not be ashamed to be yourself. Come up front and talk about everything with them. This will help them understand you better and work things out in the most positive direction. Never use such assumptions that your partner should know how you feel. Sometimes, they do know that you are hurting, but have no idea how to help you. So open up and constructively communicate your feelings without hate or mockery and watch as things become much better.

Step 8: Strive to be `Happy'; not `Right'

Happiness is not "right" all the time. I do know you are justified in your anger, but you have to make the decision to leave the feelings of righteousness and embrace happiness. You must know that relationships are all about compromises and sacrifices. Even if you are 110 percent right, to enjoy peace of mind, you will have to let go. I do not mean just physically, but emotionally and psychologically. Your peace of mind is more important than trying to prove right or wrong. Ask yourself this question "is my position on the matter getting me good results? If it's not working, then change it. Take the happy road and not the "I am right" route. Ease off the melodrama in your relationship and start striving to have only happy moments. It not only strengthens your relationship, but it also enhances your health. Why lose out on both counts to be right?

Step 9: Conflict will happen, get used to it

I have heard people talk about families that never fight. There's no such thing as such a family, the only difference is that they choose to fight their battles behind closed doors. You must have issues from time to time, it shows that you are strong together and that no one is above each other. Quarrels will come at any time, but it's your approach towards them that matters the most. Do not despair when they do come, for they will arise and there's nothing you can do to stop them. All you can control is your actions and reactions towards them as well as the type of conflicts you will have. By putting this principle into your relationship, the threats you perceive when faced with any one of them will fade giving you the ability to meet them in the right manner.

Step 10: Deal with your Emotions

Now, all you have to do is control your negative emotions and let your positive traits to soar. Wallowing in self-pity has never helped anyone in times past, and you will not be the first. Allowing anger and depression become the drive in your life means you do not like living at all. Get up and change all that ridiculous thought patterns. Decide that you will live an optimistic life, raise the bar of excellence and enjoy your life. Let love be the guiding factor in your life; turn it into a proactive behavior. Ensure that your character towards your partner is positive at all moments, whether you are in public or alone. Set standards for quality in your home and begin to reap good fruits. You only get what you work hard for, so start working it out the proper way.

Steps into better communication

So far, we have taken a personal look at things and tried to fix up your relationship from a single person's view. Now, it is time to go on the interaction level and this involves your partner. Primarily, you were the only, one that sought after this information, but it is time to share and learn from each other. You may have so far consciously helped improve your relationship by adhering to the personality principles explained above, but it is time to configure your partner into the routine to have full access to healing.

You have taken the initiative and accepted all your rights and wrongs in your relationship. It is time to understand your partner and see them in a much better light. Most often, it can be hard to indoctrinate your partner into this routine but you can try.

Many scenarios may apply; firstly, your partner may be quite aware and willing to work with you on this, if that is the case then move onto the 10-step guide. In other scenarios, your partner may not be ready to go down that part with you; they may even grow defensive and cynical. You should calm yourself and understand that all that cynicism you witness is not because they wish to hurt you but that deep down they already feel so vulnerable that they are afraid to go down that path with you. At this stage, you may decide to go on without them. You can do that, only that it's much harder when you alone are doing all the work, but it is not impossible. Resist the urge to get defensive and hurt and look at it from the bright side. In time, your conscious efforts will bring about unconscious and intuitive reactions towards a better relationship. I know it may seem a bit too hard but picture the bright better days ahead and let it help you continue on this path.

If your partner decides to join you on this journey, then it is time to reconnect and we will be doing this in 7 steps, again described by McGraw:

Step 1

Begin your dialogue with your partner by explaining how happy you are about going on this journey together. Tell them in summarized versions about all you have been doing and why you decided to do this. This dialogue should be more like a show of appreciation and not that of judgment. You can begin by saying "I decided to take this path because I wish to love you more and now I am bringing you in so I can learn better."

Step 2

Describe all the personal problems that you were able to find during this process.

Step 3

Define all you have consciously done in trying to improve your character towards loving your partner more and what you have achieved so far.

Step 4

Describe the core personal values that you both need in this relationship.

Step 5

It is time to get a bit more open. Share your personal profile of what you wish changed in your Partner, remember to be patient, humble and respectful even when your partner gets defensive towards you. Strive to take things slow; you may also let things be for a few days to allow your partner calm down.

Step 6

Share the questionnaires at the early part of this chapter with your partner and let them come up with problems they perceive on their own.

Step 7

Compare your lists with those of your partner. Keep an objective mind as some of it may hurt you. Sometimes we are not the best judges of our virtues. Try as much as possible to understand your partner's opinion about things perceived differently. This is very important to prepare you both for how best to tackle your relationship.

Priority Management

It's a whole new relationship from now henceforth, and this means an entirely new set of priorities. Your priorities must be clear and precise; this is a sort of vow to each other which shows how much your relationship is essential to each other. No relationship should be made without priorities as this gives you both a clear vision of what you want most in it and how to achieve it. Make no mistake, as you face newer challenges you will have to revisit this list from time to time because right now you may feel it is so powerful that you will not forget, but problems can make you forget, so ensure to visit this list from time to time.

Money Management

Since money fights may have been part of the issues, it's time to sort it out too. To do this, you have to sit down together and discuss your perceptions towards money. This gives a more unobstructed view of what to expect from your partner. This will help prepare you for any scenarios that may arise in future. It also gives you clarity on if a joint account is your best option or not. Once you have this view, try as much as possible to discuss how much you make each, and leave no stones unturned. Take this discussion further down on how you plan on handling all debts and bills that come by. If you plan on making a joint account, set aside an amount for domestic issues and as much as possible give each other breathing space to live a little at times.

Make sure to compromise your goals accurately and money troubles will be limited in your home. Do not make the mistake of keeping a secret stash elsewhere as this may break your relationship if it ever comes to light. If you can't seem to compromise on finance, then it's time to bring in a third party—a financial planner, there's nothing to be ashamed off, some of us prefer the third party, all the same as it lets us have time for other things. A financial planner will help give you the best budget to ensure your family stays afloat and thereby reduce all issues that can be brought about by money.

Revitalizing your sex Life

Sex is significant in your relationship and must be renewed. But Sex cannot be restored if all other aspects are not entirely worked on so you should ensure to work hard at all other factors and this will be a great extension of the renewed expression of love for each other. Some of us already have a great sex life with our partners, but no such thing as closeness and this has led us to seek refuge elsewhere. Well, let me tell you a bit of a tale; if you ignore your partner in the morning, bark at them at noon and expect a great sex life, then you are so wrong. Sex goes beyond the bed to endearments and hugs, kisses and flirtatious moments. It also goes as far as little acts of care and kindness. So for your sex life to take a new turn, you have to relate appropriately with your partner on all counts.

Sharing Domestic Responsibilities

Domestic responsibilities can destroy your relationship if not properly managed. Most often, we begin our relationships with different distribution patterns. Every responsibility in any relationship is meant to be shared equally. Women may have the ability to do more but try as much as possible to make sure you and your partner are both contributing domestically. Take out a journal and come up with a practical approach. Relationships are different everywhere, and it is possible you may not have to share chores equally, but an excellent communication can help solidify the right approach to this problem, but you must come up with the solution on paper and not leave it hanging out there as it may haunt you later.

Chapter Four

The Traits Of A Successful Couple

What's so different between your relationship and the kind of relationship you wish to have? How do you build it up? Chemistry and attraction may have brought you this far, but you need more than that to maintain a stable relationship with your partner.

You have gone through the questions and maybe you are in the process of building a better home, but you can't quite place the picture of a happy, loving home.

You may have an idea of what it looks like, but the components of that home are still entirely unclear in your head. You need this picture to work on your home, you need this qualities and traits so you can channel all that you have and all you plan to achieve towards incorporating these traits into your relationship.

Compassion

Compassion is the ability to be able to put yourself in another's shoes to empathize, that is, to understand all that is happening around the person. You must be compassionate to each other if your relationship is to work. It is a crucial ingredient to a healthy, prosperous relationship.

Compromise

The belief that lack of conflicts makes a happy home is untrue. What makes a comfortable home is actually the ability to make sacrifices for one another. Problems will arise, but knowing you can face them together, making sacrifices to accommodate each other is what counts.

A good sense of humor

Laughter is essential for healthy living, and your relationship also needs a whole lot of it. No matter the messiness of the situation, you must be able to find happiness in every little moment; this will make your relationship stronger and stop it from becoming a battle of wits.

Trust

Trust is also an essential trait of any happy relationship. Your ability to trust each other should not be based on whether your partner has cheated on you or not but should be based on a desire to enjoy peace. You must also share your thoughts with each other at all times; this solidifies trust and makes you stronger.

Optimism

We all need to feel appreciated at different times, a happy relationship is built on praises and simple statements like "thank you" or "I love you." You should complement each other at all times even in situations we find insignificant.

Intimacy

A sexual relationship is significant and so is emotional intimacy. Intimacy brings a feeling of being accepted, understood and being a part of someone's life.

Mutual respect

Happy couples admire and mutually respect each other, not just because of achievements, but because they are glad to have each other. You must respect your partner's beliefs, strengths, values, as well as flaws if you must grow together.

Friendship

Happy couples have a great rapport; they are each other's favorite company and genuinely like each other. Sometimes, they even consider each other as being best friends.

Affection

Little displays of devotion to each other are central to the life of happy couples. This serves as memoirs that they still love and cherish each other.

Reliability

Partners, who are happy with each other, rely on each other. They feel safe with themselves knowing all words and actions are appreciated by the significant other.

Understanding/communication

Happy relationships are built on openness and ability to freely express feeling to each other. They deal with issues as they arise and never try to bury anger or hurt so that they can work together more efficiently.

Chore Sharing

Happy couples enjoy each other's company so much that they are delighted sharing domestic chores and parenting together. They keep a "team" atmosphere.

Ability to make repair efforts

Happy relationships do have conflicts, and when they do, they are quite ready to take responsibilities and work together to make things better for themselves. They never give room to resentment or hatred.

Chapter Five

Hiring External Help?

No one likes the idea of spilling the beans in front of a third party. No one wants the idea that someone else fixed up their affairs. In truth, it's about you both, but sometimes this might be a quicker and safer route to get back together. It doesn't make you less capable of handling things your own way; it only saves you all that trouble to go through all that melodrama.

Sometimes, you do not need to have problems before you go into counseling; it is a delusion to say that only troubled couples go to counseling. Counseling is more than fixing up your problems, it usually involves helping you bustle a stronger relationship, the word stronger in emphasis.

Because of wrong notions, most couples only go for counseling after problems had festered and eaten an enormous hole in their relationships. This should not be your case. You can go for counseling with your partner (Partner) whether you have problems or not. In fact, it should be like a fun event where you get to renew your vows to each other.

According to explanations from various associations of counselors, counseling usually helps you benefit in three areas:

- Improved communication
- Renewing emotional connection and
- Renegotiating your commitments

Improved Communication

Our ability to communicate with each other is essential in our relationship. Even after going through all these outlined information on how to build your relationship, you may be one of the lucky few that need the help of a spectator. A counselor is trained to ensure you see eye to eye on every matter. A good counselor will take a critical view of your communication habits and gear you towards the right path. This doesn't mean you were so weak to work it out, it only means that you were too self-righteous or actually in the wrong relationship. A counselor's office will help you determine the right step to take especially when in doubt about your next approach as you are encouraged to share all information with each other without having drama involved in it.

Renewing Emotional Connection

One thing we know for sure is that using those early days of chemistry, you almost never kept your hands off each other. You were probably amazed at how much connections and bond you actually had then. Well, I do believe you can have it all again. It's natural that after been with each other for a long time, you begin to forget all those physical qualities that attracted you to each other the first time.

A counselor might critically ask you all that and more to help guide your thought patterns away from the flaws of your partner giving you a renewed interest. Emotional connections only grow with excitement and the more interested you are in your Partner, the greater the bond you share. A good counselor will guide you in that direction and helps restore physical and psychological intimacy with each other.

Renegotiating commitments

You probably made a lot of vows to each other at the beginning, but somewhere along the line, you seem to have forgotten about all that promises and pledges. We all have fears and concerns at some point which lead us away from the commitments we made to each other. These fears and concerns will be dealt with appropriately by the counselor in such an objective manner that you can view things correctly with the counselor's help.

Benefits gained from visiting a counselor cannot be overemphasized and should not be perceived as a sign of weakness. If you should visit the medical doctor for routine physical checkup or treatment, why can't you visit the psychologist equally for similar purposes?

Chapter Six

Our Stories

Case 1: Anne's Story

I met my hubby for the first time at a friend's Birthday Party on the eve of Christmas. I wouldn't say it was love at first sight but actually under the sheets at first light. We were both highly intoxicated and ended up in bed before midnight only to awaken the next morning and path awkwardly. It was the first time I ever I had such a scenario, and I was very embarrassed about it.

About 4 months later, we met again at an office luncheon launched by my firm. At first, it was so awkward for me that I avoided him at all cost until we were thrown together by my boss who wanted a contract to go through.

The conversation began from a stilted point, but soon we were laughing at funny jokes and actually enjoying each other's company.

We exchanged contacts and began to have fantastic fun holidays together, yes, only holidays for he stayed a great deal of 2 hours from me and we were both business minded so our jobs couldn't let any more time.

My friends thought I was crazy for holding onto a guy 2 hours away but he was the best thing that happened to me, and I didn't want to let go.

Two years later we were still together, and I was visiting, as usual, some days to Christmas, I remember it like it was yesterday for it was the day we had the hilarious engagement night.

We were having dinner at a Chinese restaurant when the waitress accidentally splashed some food unto his jacket. Amidst trying to clean off the stain from his coat, my engagement ring found its way into my dinner. It was so funny, exciting and stunning, all at once, to crown it all, he forgot how much food still remained on his jacket and went down on bended knees picked the ring from my noodles and proposed to me.

Several months later, I removed myself, resigned from my job and joined him in New York. I had plans to become a Wedding Event Planner and what better motivation than my own wedding. Aspirations planned, I was optimistic and looking forward to it all and I can say we had the world that first year. I can't say we had no fights and quarrels because that would be a lie, but we learned how to adjust to each other and worked out the best way to continue loving one another.

Our problems began halfway into the 3rd year of our Marriage with the death of my husband's sister. She committed suicide leaving us all quite desolate. The coming months put a lot of strain on our marriage. Dave grew cold towards me; I didn't quite understand what led to her death. When I tried having conversations with my husband, I was instantly stonewalled, or he would lash out and walk out of the house. With time, he began coming home very late at night, all boozed up. I kept telling myself "it is all a phase, it will soon pass away." Soon my husband began having alcohol for breakfast, lunch, and dinner and after a while, he lost his job.

Our young daughter, Charlotte, grew scared of him and found a way to avoid him at all costs which only infuriated him much more.
One night, he came home, all drunk as usual, but this time it was different, he bore the telltale signs of adultery. I had gotten enough of it all and couldn't bear it any longer, I lashed out at him, and we had the worst quarrel that went beyond words to his using his belt on me.

Amidst it all, I lost consciousness and was rushed to the hospital. That day, I lost our second baby, and I decided I was done, I wasn't going back anymore.

I moved in with one of my colleagues (which were quite humiliating).

For several months he tried to contact me, but I refused. I even went as far as filing for a divorce.

One morning, my hubby turned up at the entrance of my office with the most prominent bouquet of flowers I had ever seen. I know instinctively that this time was different. I accepted to have a date with him, but most surprising all he wanted was a lunch date at a different part of town.

Lunch happened in the office of a Psychologist which was actually a first for me. For the first time since we came to be together, I saw my husband for who he really was. My husband and his sister had been subject to sexual abuse during childhood. Yes, he had moved beyond that, but his sister's death opened the wounds so hastily closed up.

Today, we are blessed with 3 kids and have been together ever since, and it still feels like we married anew. Who knew that we will be together 25 years after still having our wedding anniversaries at a Chinese restaurant?

Case 2: Kate and Danny

I met Danny in high school. We became so inseparable and hanged out more often, and soon everyone planned our wedding long before we took that step. As predicted, we got married few months after high school; I got a job as a waitress while he becomes a delivery man at the local grocery store. We were so young, living on our own with only little to eat and a roof over our head for the first time in life and to crown it all we were terribly optimistic and happy.

For months on end, we enjoyed each other's company, our quarrels only lasted minutes, and I had the perfect man. Then Dave got into Medical school, I was so happy he was pursuing his dreams. At that time I was pregnant with our first child. We began having issues with our finances, there were textbooks to buy, food and all else but we retained our optimism despite all else.

At the beginning of the second year in Med School, problems erupted. Dave and I began to fight on a daily basis, he kept late nights, and I started to suspect he was having an affair. But between the responsibilities of handling our child and waitressing, I could find no clues whatsoever about the incident.

One night, we had a party with his friends after exams, it was such a beautiful sight, I got to see my man in his full glory, he was so brilliant, and I loved every bit of the discussions around me, but I couldn't contribute to it. Then I decided to give it a go and add my opinions to the discussion on the ground. I can never forget the look they all gave me as if I was too dumb to comprehend their view. The worst of it all; My Danny looked to me as if I were uneducated. That night we had the worst rows than we ever had before.

Several months after that, I received an email containing images of my beloved husband and his newfound catch, my daring best friend, and confidant having an excellent time with my soul mate. It was the height of betrayal from my husband. I decided it was time to make a move out which I did, I quit my job as a Waitress, took out all of our savings and moved out of state with our 3-year-old child. I was too hurt and angry to even comprehend seeing him one more time.

For several months, we stayed apart, each to its own aspirations. I successfully enrolled in evening business school and got myself a career, but I was embittered and did not wish to be around any man. My husband, on the other hand, continued his affair with his mistress for several months.

We met again as total strangers at a funeral of a loved one in the neighborhood of our town. And there we began a friendship that later blossomed into our being together again. After a full year and a half apart, we moved to a new home and city and built a brand new house based on different principles and with added levels of maturity.

We recently celebrated 12 years of marriage, and even with my failing health, I can say that I am blessed with a beautiful family. We love deeper, forgive easier, communicate and serve as support to each other.

At a time during the breakup, I would have quickly rebuked anyone who tried to say that we would find each other again, but today, I am glad we did.

Case 3: Jake's Story

I met my life on a flight to Oklahoma many years day ago. I remember that day like it was yesterday, a beautiful sweet angel smiling down at me. At first, I thought I was in heaven, but then she brought the refreshments up to my line of view, and we laughed. I guess I had made a comment as much, so she knew what I was thinking. Well, I began having a lot of coffees at the Airport in a bid to catch a glimpse of my angel each time she came into town.

After several nights together, she told me she was quitting her job for something better in my town. I was so happy; things were finally working in my direction. Well, I was so pleased that I suggested she move in with me. This she did, and I can rightly say we had a lot of fun together. Seven months later, we took to Court and got married. Little did I know that all were not as it seemed.

About three months into our married, I found my wife at a restaurant with some random guy. When I confronted her about it, she got furious, that it was all business and that my fears were unjustified. As a middle-aged man, with no physically attractive quality, I always had concerns that I got married to someone way higher than me, for she was so stunningly beautiful.

A year into our marriage, I took a trip to Oklahoma on business, but the workshop I was attending got canceled at the last minute, so I returned a day earlier, and the sight that greeted me in my home was terrible. My wife was in bed with our Gardener. It was such a terrible experience, and I wasted no time in moving out that night. I was so hurt that I didn't want to set my eyes on her at all. I knew our sex life was so limited, but I never knew it could bring this kind of trouble. On investigations, I uncovered more and more philandering activities by my wife.

I told myself "I was done with it all and then I moved out of our neighborhood so that I would never want to walk into her by chance or whatever.

Eight months later, I became an embittered young man sampling every pie out there on the streets and to crown it all, I still missed my wife and what made it worse is that she kept sending me memoirs on how sorry she was until I had to tell my secretary to filter my messages, so I did not see any of them.

On the eve of Thanksgiving, My wife paid me a visit to an office luncheon held by my Company (someone in my office apparently helped her out). She looked as beautiful as ever, and I couldn't find a way to say 'No' to her.

We talked a lot that night, and by the next day, we were back at home together and have been together ever since.

Recently, we visited Africa to celebrate our 30 years in marriage. So much fun and here I am wondering what my life would have become without her. I know it would have been really terrible!

Conclusion

Everyone has a story to tell at some point in life. Some so heartbreaking and yet others give us the life lessons to incorporate into our relationships.

The difference, therefore, is how yours ends and not its beginning. In this struggle for a healthy and happy relationship, I hope you have found the perfect strategy to enjoy your life as well as have a fulfilling companionship with your partner.

The morals then are never to be ashamed of your relationship, pursue it and give it all the intensity and hard work. Take pride in your partner, explore every angle of your relationship, develop and practice all it requires. Never be afraid to enjoy yourself throughout this journey, you deserve it. Do not waste time or energy on negative emotions that not only ruin your relationship but give you medical issues with your heart. Love freely as this is your most significant gift not just to you and your partner but to humanity.

You have prepared, its time you claimed victory.

I do wish for you that your love life is fulfilling and that you derive strength from it.

About TheAauthor

Susan Howard (born 1979) is an American writer, performer and social media expert, born, and raised in Los Angeles, who lives and works in New York. Her writing includes mostly blogs, articles, and eBooks related to social media, modern living and urban life. She is focused on practical support to young generations, explaining modern phenomena in the most understandable way in order to help people to achieve a better life in different aspects.

One Last Thing

If you enjoyed this book or found it useful I'd be very grateful if you'd post a short review on Amazon. Your support really does make a difference and I read all the reviews personally, so I can get your feedback and make this book even better.

Thanks again for your support!

Please send me your feedback at

www.urbanlife.tips

Made in the
USA
Monee, IL

15844371R00039